FROM THE D...
NIA BOUDREA...

How Quickly

I Realized I HATE My Job

A Novella by

SHAMEEKA AYERS

PARAMIND PUBLICATIONS
A *Shift* in Thinking

ParaMind Publications

Copyright ©2012 by Shameeka Ayers

Published by ParaMind Publications, LLC
2090 Baker Road, Ste. 304-171, Kennesaw, Georgia 30144

Library of Congress Control Number: 2012905467

ISBN 978-0-9762738-9-9

Printed in the United States of America

www.paramindpublications.com

Cover Design
Copyright ©2012
By: Melanie Hernquist for Lucky + Lovely

Author Photography
By: Bessie Akuba

This novella is dedicated to those who *think* they are held captive by golden handcuffs and oh-so-drab gray cubicles.

Contents

The *Instantly!* Job Resignation Test . . . 71

CHAPTER

✳ ———————— ✳

1

Via Instant Messenger:

[17:12] **Nia:** "You there?"
[17:12] **Harper:** "Hellllllloooooooooo!"
[17:12] **Nia:** "I am clearly too brilliant for this place."
[17:13] **Harper:** "Well…that's a statement of the obvious."
[17:13] **Nia:** "*Le sigh* I want out, but I'm riddled with burdens such as a mortgage, groceries, and a sick shopping habit."
[17:13] **Harper:** "Oh yes…there is the matter of that last one. Your penchant for Louboutins probably can't be satisfied if you quit."
[17:14] **Nia:** "Why must you be so right?"

If Harper and I'd had this virtual conversation once over the past six months, we'd had it a million times. It had become our "thing". You know…complaining about the old 9-to-5, our very own ball-and-chain which had nothing to do with our husbands—simply the J-O-B. Truth be told, we were the millennial versions of Dolly Parton, Lily Tomlin and Jane Fonda rolled into two witty, cerebral and occasionally snarky co-workers who had become friends. Haughtiness in tow, somehow or another, we'd self-elevated to the pinnacle of the office food chain: the cool people.

Harper and I couldn't have been more different if we tried. She was a suburban, newlywed WASP with a private school background and a fancy degree in Art History with honors, no doubt (think Charlotte York from *Sex and The City* or socialite Olivia Palermo from MTV's reality show, *"The City"*). I, a BAP (you know, a *Black American Princess*), nearly 10 years her senior with a much more humble rural pedigree, was considered middle management and on my fifth stop in stuffy Corporate America.

I arrived at Taking Chances!, our employer which managed the foundations of philanthropists and corporations, Harper had been there nearly a year. Assigned a cubicle in 1/6 of the depressing chunk of space that she'd already settled into, I immediately thought her to be adorable yet mysterious. Athletically built with blonde locks, she was the picture of J Crew perfection. Her cubicle was decorated 'just so'. Pictures of her then-fiancee, high school chums and bow-headed sorority sisters peppered the putty-hued industrial walls of her space. Recently out of college, Harper was determined to make it seem that designer Kelly Wearstler had fashioned in the interior of her cube, so help her God.

I, consequently, was fresh from the devastation of a lay-off. Had you looked up the definition of 'jaded' in *Webster's*, my confused mug and furled brow would have stared right back at you. Why? So glad you asked. Before accepting the position at Taking Chances!, I'd been a Senior Account Executive at a public relations firm. Man! I loved that job…the clients, the perks, the colleagues. While all of that's awesome alone, the best thing about the former position was the luxury of telecommuting full-time. Oh, to have a commute that included a one minute "drive" from one side of my house to the other was glorious! You should have seen my litter of bunny slippers, the only wardrobe that I absolutely had to buy for four years! Le sigh, sure enough.

Though you likely won't be surprised, let me opine about how much I absolutely, positively loathe cubicles. Who invented cubicles? That rat bastard should be choked! No…shanked! No… choked AND shanked! Seriously. Whoever said cubes are akin to a farm for lab rats was on the money. Ring *that* bastard up and give him a gajillion dollars. For I cannot think of anything delightful to say about cubicles: never have, never will.

If you never do another thing for me, please, please, please imagine my horror when the Taking Chances! office manager, Mona, escorted me to my square of space on my inaugural day as a TC! employee. Mona, a middle-aged woman deeply-rooted in the glory of the 1980's (Mom jeans, tweed blazer and all), had mastered the art of office orchestration and operations: phone lists, seating charts, office supplies and the like. It was apparent that Mona had earned the role as the office drill sergeant. Her gait was regimented and her head, burdened with the weight of an atrocious bun, held high.

"Nia, this is your cube! Welcome!" she said proudly as she flashed a grin.

"Yay!" I managed to say with half of my heart. For as swift as Mona thought herself to be, I detected her somewhat retarded nature quickly. *"She actually thinks I'm glad to be here"*, I thought to myself. Mental note: someone, please kill me. Now.

Mona began the formality of introductions to those who sat in my immediate vicinity: My "block" (Doesn't it sound so…so…. correctional? Right.) was comprised of Carla, the sweet, white trash girl; Elle, the free-spirited hippie; Lucy, the requisite, Old Maid/ Plain Jane (yes, she's sadly both) and, finally, my dear, dear Harper.

What I loved most about Harper is that she wasn't overbearing; I hate when people come on too strongly. Grrr. For nearly six months she and I exchanged the occasional pleasantry and interacted only when professionally necessary; read: we were each watching the stylish moves of the other very, very closely.

Not much of a friend-seeker at work, I basically arrived on time, performed my duties and punched out directly at 5:30 PM, all the while keeping to myself. You see, I'd learned through the office grapevine that the Divine Miss Harper had gained the reputation of being somewhat a snob (sorry if you didn't know this already, Harp) and could be standoff-ish. Since it takes a snob to know one, I equally and occasionally snubbed Harper even whilst she planned her grand, Trump Family-esque wedding from the comfort of her cube and fended off her minions who stopped by for all of the shower updates (because there were, like, *fifty* pre-wedding parties) and ceremony details. *Who cares?* I thought as she shoo-ed off her wannabe handmaidens. *Do Harper and her crew ever do any work?,* I just couldn't help but wonder.

Truth be told, I did not see much of Harper for a couple of summer months after that. For one, she was off getting married on Nantucket and, secondly, she spent nearly another few weeks honeymooning with her newly betrothed, Kent, in (you guessed it) the South. Of. Freaking. France.

Hate her.

CHAPTER

※ ——————— *※*

2

Though I'd only been there a short while, my days at Taking Chances! had mutated and grown as long as a country mile. The levels of disorganization, dysfunction and managerial ineptitude absolutely amazed me.

If Candid Camera had done a feature on me, my eyes were probably glazed over as soon as I hit week #2 on the staff. The company, which might have seemed to be solid to an outsider, was an utter mess. Saying that it had run amok would be a tremendous understatement.

Oh, dear! Where shall I begin? Executive designations were bestowed to employees based on tenure rather than talent. If that weren't enough, there was no Human Resources professional to whom a puzzled employee might expect to address any problems or challenges. With a confirmed frat boy at the helm, Taking Chances! was high on fun but low on expectations and accountability.

Since a majority of the employees were under the age of thirty, the social committee offered a rotating portfolio of after-hours events. Whatever dollars saved by not compensating their employees based on their expertise were invested in coolers and coolers and coolers and coolers of beer supplemented by vats and vats and vats and vats of wine. The consumption of alcohol in the office (yes, in the office) had me raise the occasional eyebrow but since even snobs can have the affinity for a "cold one", I was happy to indulge.

There was no science to recruitment of staff at Taking Chances! With a handful exceptions (storyteller definitely being excluded, thank you), the following criteria was the prototype for the ideal employee: Cute? Check. Ability to walk and chew gum? Check. Willing to work for peanuts? Check. You're hired! Hey, this strategy seemed to work for the company, and if it ain't broke, why fix it?

You see, Taking Chances! was like a ponzi scheme. Friends lured other friends into the incestuous fold except there was no incentive such as a referral bonus. Are you shocked?! Didn't I tell you how cheap they were?

The friend that is an existing employee spins glorious tales of how wonderful, fun, exciting and fabulous the Taking Chances! organization has proven to be. Then they gush about its President, Barry, and the darling Vice-Presidents, Meagan and Sarah, who have all been with the company for over a decade. High on your friend's supply, you actually become excited and submit your resume. Within a week or so, you talk to a couple of people, and before you know it, you're hired!

My up-line in the pyramid was my old friend, Melanie.

"Oh, Taking Chances! is great!" she said.

"It's the kind of work environment that we're used to," proclaimed she. Being a former colleague from the PR firm, she was well aware of my corporate culture expectations. After all, she'd been an employee at Taking Chances! for nearly six months herself.

Because I knew Melanie so well, I knew she wouldn't lead me astray when asked if she could throw my name in the mix for a newly created senior manager position.

When I'd been with the company for about a month and began to notice the craziness, I tugged Melanie's hemline at lunch one day.

"Mel, can I ask you something?"

"Sure," she answered between bites of her favorite garlic shrimp pasta.

"Is it me or is this place whack? I mean, there are no policies and procedures, the wrong people seem to be in the wrong roles, and no one seems to care! This is crazy!"

And with the fury of a thousand angry tongues, Melanie spilled months and months of frustration and disenchantment smack dab in my lap. Her complaints and concerns mirrored mine—one after the other. Despite working in another division of the company, she hated her job. Let me correct myself: if only there was a disposition stronger than hate, it would likely be more appropriate. Maybe 'loathed' was the better fit. Melanie felt micro-managed and was generally annoyed by her direct supervisor, Sarah, who spent her days doing anything that anyone could actually pinpoint.

"Yeah, what does Sarah *really* do?" I quizzed.

The blank look on her face said it all, but Melanie took it a step further. "She does nothing and gets away with it because Taking Chances! is fucked up."

My heart sank as I sat across from Melanie absolutely dumbfounded by what seemed to be a fatal mistake: this job.

As much as I love a fresh, gigantic Caesar salad topped with grilled chicken, I instantaneously lost my appetite and wasted twelve dollars. I could not stomach another bite.

All I could manage to think (and I know it's not ladylike) was: *Oh, shit.*

Sorry, Mom.

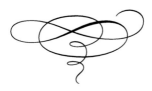

CHAPTER

3

While the days at Taking Chances! were mostly annoying, I decided to stick it out and make every attempt possible to do a bang-up job. Never a fan of job-hopping or short stints on my resumé, I busied myself with projects and responsibilities in order to distract myself from the general dysfunction of the company's operations.

Autumn, a historically active fundraising season for our client foundations, had dawned upon us, and I was busier than a one-legged man in a butt-kicking contest. There were $10,000 per plate dinners to plan, reports to generate and presentations to give. I could not be bothered by the minutiae of office gossip and politics. I was there to do my job, it's really that simple. I resigned myself to this notion:

as long as Taking Chances! payroll checks cleared my bank account every two weeks, they were OK with me.

Meanwhile, preening in a cubicle near mine, Harper had long since returned from her luxurious honeymoon. She had properly handwritten all of her thank you notes, meticulously selected all of her wedding photos from the proofs delivered to the office by her photographer's courier and settled nicely into her new abode with Kent. She was actually looking forward to getting back to work.

While Harper was basking on Cote d'Azur, our manager, Milton, decided that it'd be a great idea if Harper shadowed me on a couple of projects and further insisted that she join us at EXCITE, the annual trade show for fundraising professionals in San Francisco. The more the merrier, huh?

As Milton and I wrapped up our weekly status meeting, he was quick to broach the subject of bringing Harper up to speed.

"Nia, since Harper's old manager has resigned, I think I'll assign her to more of your projects as your back-up," he said.

"Harper's a really bright girl." Milton continued.

Somewhat annoyed by Milton's reference to an adult woman as a "girl", I mentally filed his mis-step and agreed to set up a meeting with Harper to discuss projects, expectations and our looming sojourn to the Left coast.

Because I ran a casual (but tight) ship, I decided to pow-wow with Harper on a Friday morning. Not to be deterred by cubicles, I scheduled our meeting in one of the company's executive board rooms. Harper showed up in a wrap cashmere sweater, Joe's Jeans and Burberry riding boots. All business, she took careful notes on the steno pad in her folio. She shared her expertise, asked the right questions and rattled the litany of action items right back at me.

I felt somewhat horrible because I'd *soooooooooo* pre-judged Harper. I must do better. For all of the prima-donna flack that she'd gotten from some of the jealous girls in the office (in the 'hood, they are called "haters"), she was actually quite pleasant. Her parents would be thrilled to know that she was a gem even. Dare I say that I usually don't like that many people? Color me a malcontent.

But as I was getting to know her, Harper definitely struck a chord with me.

As we wrapped up the meeting by exchanging weekend plans (she and Kent were attending a football game at his alma mater and my husband, Evan, and I would be experiencing Friday Night Lights at my stepson's Varsity football game), Harper spun around on her heels with an afterthought.

"Do you I-M?"

CHAPTER

4

A flag-waving, Gen-Xer, I prided myself on being attune to all things technology-based and productivity tool-centric yet, alas, was a virgin to the world of instant messaging. Ashamed that I'd had to admit that it was a foreign concept to Harper on the previous Friday, I asked if she would set up some time in our Outlook™ calendars for an instant messaging tutorial. Before I knew it, Harper was giving me a comprehensive primer on the art of being able to communicate in real-time but not being burdened with the formality of an e-mail.

"Nia, you'll pick this up in no time," she assured me.

Just short of sweating beads, I wondered if I looked *that* nervous. I'd recently turned thirty-five years old and was already feeling a bit antiquated in the sea of young whippersnappers at Taking Chances!, so I wasn't very optimistic. My furled brow obviously gave me away.

"Seriously. Just relax," she said. "If you use text messaging on your cell phone, it's very similar."

"Do you have a Google™ or Yahoo™ account?" she asked.

I nodded. Obviously, the fear had turned me into a speechless idiot.

"OK, great! If you'll pull it up, we can get your IM activated right now. This will be great because if we have a quick question for each other about the projects that we share, all we have to do is use IM. A lot of people in the office use it!"

In about five minutes, Harper had me all squared away.

She scooted back to her cube and before I knew it, I got the following message from her:

[16:46] **Harper:** testing, testing, testing
[16:46] **Nia:** hello!
[16:46] **Harper:** ok...you're all set!
[16:47] **Nia:** thanks for hooking an old lady up! we're going to have a blast together. I can see it already.
[16:47] **Harper:** ;-)...lol

What in the hell is lol (pronounced 'lawl" in my head)? I wondered. Le sigh. Ah, the generational divide was becoming oh-so-apparent.

With the trip to San Francisco just a couple of weeks away, Harper and I were preparing marketing kits (assembly line and all...ugh!), ordering promotional items and fine-tuning our sales schpiels. 'Twas my first trip to the Bay Area and Harper had an old college friend there, so each of us was motivated beyond our professional responsibilities and awaited the trip with bated breath.

As Harper and I realized that we were really a good team and worked so well together, some of the formality in our relationship began to disappear. Instant messaging had really helped us a lot as we forged through our shared deliverables. I had been converted! *Hallelujah!*

One afternoon, we took a working lunch to make a jaunt to Office Depot™ to grab final presentation binders for our trip. As we were awaiting a green light, Harper looked over to me from behind the wheel of her convertible Volkswagen New Beetle and asked with a straight face:

"You hate it don't you? You don't have to answer me now. Taking Chances! is full of loser ass, subterranean losers and you're different. I know you are. There I said it."

I don't remember if I was more surprised by her chutzpah or if my loss of words came from the knees of my six feet tall body nearly caving in my chest when Harper quickly hung a left through the changed light. I suppose a lesser woman would have stiffened her upper lip and shot a quick, "Why, what ever do you mean?" right back at Harper. But I didn't. I couldn't.

Instantly (Get it? Of course you do! Ha!), I quickly realized that as completely different as Harper and I were on the surface, we were actually kindred spirits: utter coolness (*duh!*), style, food, reality TV and the list goes on. Who knew?

At that moment, any semblance of a façade crumbled and all we could do was laugh.

And laugh. And laugh. And laugh. We'd found our most common denominator: the hatred of Taking Chances! In the twinkle of an eye, we'd formed an unspoken sisterhood that would bind us eternally (or at least between 9 and 5 every day).

CHAPTER

⸺⸺⸺⸺

5

After the comparison of our "Top 10 Reasons Why Working at Taking Chances! Sucks" lists, Harper and I became thicker than Ali Baba and his gang of thieves. Knowing that someone else was agitated, annoyed and bewildered by the cast of characters at Taking Chances! made it easier for me to get out of bed each morning, shower, slip on my Jimmy Choos and show up with a smirk. Trust me: Taking Chances! was not worth a full smile.

Since Mona had hastily suspended the office's coffee service (something about this budgetary cut being worth four hundred *measly* dollars per year), Harper and I began to take turns popping into Starbucks for two tall, skinny mocha lattes. Who needed to rely on Taking Chances! for a cup of joe anyway? Definitely not us. There was no way we'd remotely make it through the day without a jolt of caffeine. Our days begin by dropping a cup of coffee to the other (while saying "Good Morning" and executing the universal sign language of a gun blowing your brains out), settling in our horrible cubicles, scanning our inboxes for any urgent, work-related emails, and then logging into Yahoo™ Instant Messenger.

Now that I'd finally gotten the swing of instant messaging, not one single thing was off limits. The technology was sure enough productive for work but it also brought out the little devil that rests on my shoulders. Same for Harper. All of the things that we thought about and observed about our Taking Chances! colleagues as we toiled away in our dreadful cubicles became fair game.

The silver lining? We we worked with such colossal, world-class losers that we never ran short on fodder.

[09:29] **Harper:** please tell me you have seen Mona's outfit this morning!
[09:31] **Nia:** 'Morning! Where are your manners? LOL!
[09:31] **Harper:** Good morning!
[09:31] **Nia:** Ummmmm...how could I not? Even Stevie Wonder can see that poncho.
[09:31] **Harper:** hahahahaha
[09:31] **Nia:** Maybe I shouldn't have told her it was cute.
[09:31] **Harper:** dying!
[09:31] **Harper:** she might make you one now
[09:32] **Nia:** That's what I'm afraid of...damn!
[09:32] **Harper:** watch out!
[09:32] **Nia:** She prob spent the weekend crocheting more
[09:32] **Nia:** Perhaps I should at least bring my own yarn and head her off at the pass.
[09:32] **Harper:** LOL! good idea!
[09:32] **Harper:** Memo to Mona: neon is OUT unless it's 1982 and you're desperately seeking Susan.

[09:33] **Nia:** for that matter, ponchos are out!
[09:33] **Nia:** for everyone except Mona and her student of fashion, a one Willie (note: another one of our colleagues)
[09:34] **Harper:** maybe she can make Willie a denim one
[09:35] **Nia:** bwahahahaha...now that'd be funny

Willie, whose government name was Wilhelmina, was Taking Chances!' Director of Information Technology. Harper and I bestowed "Willie" upon her because she made us feel weird whenever she came around; giving us what else, but the Willies, the world renowned, skin-crawling sensation. Willie was the leader of a motley crew of anti-social application developers, web designers and network administrators who were her superiors intellectually, but cow-towed to her mammy-style grumbling and finger-waving. Willie was almost always attitudinal and spoke in quixotic dialect which Harper and I called JibberJabber.

Technologically inept (hell, why should the Director of IT actually have to know anything about technology?), she spent her days marching through the cubicles' main thoroughfare huffing and puffing like she was going to blow the office park down. We suspected that it was actually easier for her to complain and manufacture drama than to confess her lack of managerial and professional acumen.

"These folks are getting on my nerves!" she sighed.

"I don't have time for all of this" she blew.

"These folks are getting on my nerves. Still.",she complained once more.

Willie never made the proclamations listed above to any one particular co-worker, she simply spewed them out to whoever might listen. Oh, how passive-aggressive was she! Well surprise, surprise and welcome to the halls of Taking Chances!, where not having the cohunes to 'say what you mean and mean what you say' was a recurring theme.

Willie, who looked like she was separated at birth from Good Times' Esther Rolle a.k.a. Florida Evans, was a throwback through and through. Surely upon this notion, she and Mona forged a friendly alliance and Complainer's Consortium. On strolls between cubes, we found, they even relied heavily on each other for fashion advice. Harper and I were frightened for them both.

[17:13] **Harper:** oh dear, Willie is getting fashion advice from Mona
[17:15] **Nia:** OMG
[17:15] **Nia:** Say it ain't so!
[17:16] **Nia:** This is a case study of The Blind Leading the Blind
[17:16] **Harper:** yes, and there was mention of leather
[17:16] **Nia:** Hush your mouth!
[17:16] **Nia:** Dialing up Stacy London right now!
[17:16] **Harper:** please do!
[17:16] **Nia:** There is an atrocity lingering...
[17:16] **Nia:** Some people, I've decided, are hopeless.
[17:17] **Nia:** Willie and Mona will spontaneously combust in their leather/pleather.
[17:17] **Harper:** haha

It probably goes without saying that Willie was no-way, no-how a fashion plate. One of her favorite outfits was the abominable combination of a denim jacket with denim jeans. I imagine that some time long-ago and in a far, far such this mix was fashionable. Oh, yes...like NEVER! Give me a break! This was a fashion faux mis-step of epic proportion in my book. Willie usually wore this get-up every Friday and it offended the sensibilities of the fashion-conscious in her path each and every time. Harper and I were no exception.

[11:29] **Nia:** So Willie is wearing a denim tuxedo today
[11:29] **Harper:** It's a Friday; so what else is new?
[11:29] **Harper:** seriously, where are Stacy and Clinton of TLC's "What Not To Wear?"
[11:30] **Harper:** They could film a whole season if they stopped by our office and filmed some of these fashion misfits.
[11:30]**Nia:** bwahahaahaha but crying on the inside.
[11:31]**Harper:** Do please tell why you're crying inside THIS time?
[11:31]**Nia:** I hate these losers. I hate my life. I hate my job.
[11:32]**Harper:** Oh, is that all?

Having hired a full time receptionist, Willie's sidekick, Mona, had recently taken a cubicle in our general vicinity. Though she didn't spend a great deal actually sitting, she made our lives a living hell when she was! She spent her days "negotiating" reduced prices for manila folders and push pins using her "outside" voice. Not only was Mona annoying, she also managed to be inconsiderate. Surely no one had passed her the book on cubicle etiquette (note to self: pen that tome next). It wasn't that we were doing so much powerful work that couldn't be disturbed. We were most annoyed by the way Mona attempted to man-handle various and sundry customer service representatives on the other end of the phone. She was a condescending know-it-all. Those of us who sat around her witnessed her smug nature on more than one occasion. Since she was a guppy in the office's social hierarchy, her demands did not fly with the Taking Chances! staff. If arguing with the copier salesman made her feel more powerful, she was eager for such the heated exchange.

[17:14] **Harper:** Mona, shut it! I can't focus on reading Facebook.
[17:15] **Nia:** I can't get beyond her outfit enough to listen. I am somewhat mesmerized by the fact that Mona is wearing jodhpurs. At work.

[17:15] **Harper:** Where do you buy something like that?
[17:15] **Nia:** they are so wrong that they are enchanting
[17:15] **Nia:** like, i can't stop looking
[17:15] **Harper:** much like the train wreck that they are
[17:15] **Nia:** yeah fascinating
[17:16] **Harper:** does her blazer have patches on the elbows?
[17:16] **Harper:** Damn skippy! Mona does like to dress in the horse genre
[17:16] **Nia:** perhaps she was an equestrian in another life; hence the long ponytail which she coils into that God-awful chignon?
[17:16] **Nia:** *le sigh*
[17:16] **Harper:** When do we leave for San Fran? I'm over these losers at the office for a while?
[17:16] **Nia:** Not soon enough. I need a break, too.
[17:16] **Harper:** Dear God. Please let us survive San Fran lest I be jailed at Alcatraz for being annoyed by work people (present company excluded, of course)
[17:17] **Nia:** Oh. Thanks for sparing me. You're too kind.
[17:17] **Nia:** Here's to Alcatraz!
[17:17] **Harper:** Cheers, doll!

CHAPTER

6

The trip to San Francisco was the first opportunity that our newly formed team had traveled together on business. From Milton to Harper to me, everyone was a tad wet behind the ears. In fact, now that I think about it, Harper had the most seniority.

It'd be interesting to see how we interacted beyond the office.

Joining us at EXCITE, were also two terribly, terribly, terribly annoying colleagues. Now I am the first to admit, my feathers are easily ruffled; especially when it comes to brown-nosing, do-gooders. I am trying to be more tolerant. Please pray for me.

Enter Sherri Hinder and Tina Patchouli.

A couple of months before our trip, Milton used the Taking Chances! recruitment strategy (you know, amongst other things, "Can you walk and chew gum?") to fill a critical position within our team, Manager of Public Affairs.

After rounds and rounds of panel-styled interviews, it was apparent to most of us staffers that Sherri Hinder (aka 'The Hinderance') might not be a good fit for our team. For such an integral and visible role, Sherri seemed to be void the necessary luster and confidence to act as our clients' media envoy. Our feedback to Milton was consistent; she shook like a leaf throughout the interviews and appeared to be a bundle of nerves. When someone on the panel asked Sherri what she did in her spare time, she droned on and on about the two Pomeranians that she'd rescued...for thirty minutes. Great. She's a rambler. Not exactly Public Information Officer material, but what do I know? Since Milton fancied himself to be a great judge of skill and character, he'd drafted an offer letter before Sherri could make it back home to her dogs.

[9:26] **Harper:** Is it just me, or would this lady make the worst marketing person ever?
[9:26] **Nia:** How can the loser-ing-est person be in charge of marketing? Isn't there a creative element to it?
[9:26] **Nia:** I'll never get it.

Tina Patchouli (aka 'The Patch'), Taking Chances!'s Fundraising Manager was the anti-Sherri: very cocky, overly confident and the Queen of Appearing Busy. Many of her days were spent preening up and down and up and down the cubicle aisles generating meaningless conversations versus cold-calling on our clients' behalf. The Patch was full of glittering generalities when it came to the reports of her projects' status and her mere presence was painful at best.

[10:35] **Nia:** Not that you care but I need to say this to someone:

[10:35] **Nia:** Tina has been in Milton's office for the past hour.

[10:35] **Harper:** OMG she is in there constantly

[10:35] **Nia:** No wonder he can't answer email.

[10:35] **Harper:** hahah i know!

[10:35] **Harper:** what can they possibly be talking about

[10:35] **Nia:** Does she not have anything to do?

[10:36] **Nia:** They've been talking about Sherri Hinder the whole time.

[10:36] **Harper:** oh...

[10:36] **Nia:** The Patch has been chomping at the bit to give him her feedback.

[10:36] **Nia:** I mean...she just goes in there and camps out.

[10:36] **Harper:** The Patch is a loser!

[10:36] **Harper:** Maybe she should just move her desk in there

[10:36] **Nia:** <sigh>I digress

One of the great mysteries surrounding The Patch was (and I'll bet you can guess) her sexuality. Though she had a girl's name and boobs, she and Pat from *Saturday Night Live* had been separated at birth. Her Pat-ish, mocha-colored, naturally curly Afro was the most heinous you've ever seen. Frosted with golden highlights, the 'fro was mesmerizing and enchanting. The Patch regularly draped her pear-shaped physique with a collection of last season's dress shirts from Lauren by Ralph Lauren and a rainbow coalition of corduroy pants. Not a good look. She appeared to be the poster child for lesbians. While The Patch never mentioned a husband or a boyfriend, before long, she let the existence of her "special friend" be known. Though she was forever nebulous about her relationships outside of work, she and her "special friend" just so-happened to be hanging out in the Midtown (read: gay central) area of town during Gay Pride weekend and any time The Indigo Girls were striking up a live concert. Mmmhmmmm... Who was The Patch trying to hoodwink?

Certainly not Harper and me! You see, while it was certainly her right, The Patch was a corporate lesbian and not out of the closet at work. I think it would have been easier to like her if she weren't such a poseur. What ever happened to "We're here. We're queer. Get used to it?"

Harper and The Patch were on the same flight to San Francisco, I was following them on a separate flight a few hours later because I have this policy: I do not fly with people from work. That's simple enough. In the rare occasion that a colleague happens to book a seat on my flight, I do everything within my might to ensure that we do not sit closely to each other on the plane. Color me hateful, but I definitely didn't want to be bothered by a single Taking Chances! loser at fifty-thousand feet. When I'm on a plane, my goal is to relax and prepare for arrival at my final destination. My meditation and breathing exercises need not be interrupted by small talk.

As I was putting the final touches on my packing at home, my iPhone began to buzz with reckless abandon. Evan, my husband, glanced at it and passed it my way.

"It's your girl! She just sent you a text," he announced.

"Who?" I replied.

"Who else? Harper. Do you think something is going wrong with the trip? You might want to take this."

"I hate this job" I mumbled.

[5:21] **Harper:** Nia! OMG!

[5:21] **Nia:** What's wrong?! Is everything OK?

[5:22] **Harper:** I am about to die!

[5:22] **Nia:** Get to it, why don't you! You're making me nervous!

[5:23] **Harper:** It's The Patch! She is wearing a tie-dyed, Jerry Garcia shirt on the plane to San Fran. Doesn't she know 'work people' will see her and she'll be outed?

[5:24] **Harper:** Why didn't she wear something more approp? Like one of her man shirts.

[5:24] **Nia:** Why are you worrying me with this? Though it is hilarious.

[5:24] **Harper:** Please come to the gate and resuscitate me. I can't believe it.

[5:25] **Nia:** Shall I break this down for you?

[5:25] **Harper:** Don't you always have to, Sensei?

[5:25] **Nia:** I don't know how you don't get it? Haven't I taught you anything over these past couple of months?

[5:27] **Harper:** Hurry. About to board.

[5:27] **Nia:** The Patch is headed to one of the most gay-friendly cities in the world: San Francisco. That shirt is her way of saying: "Honey! I'm home!" Please give The Patch her space: She is going to her Mother Land.

[5:29] **Harper:** *falling out from laughter*

[5:29] **Nia:** I knew you would be, Grasshopper. Though Milton will certainly say something to annoy you, please don't shank anyone before I arrive.

[5:30] **Harper:** I'll try but I can't promise.

We all arrived in San Francisco safely. Harper was a bit more annoyed than I because of her mis-step in booking the same flight as Milton, The Patch and The Hinderance. A cab ride with this trio didn't exactly scream fun. After checking into the swanky Clift Hotel, the four of us planned to meet in the lobby and go out for a staff dinner in preparation for manning our booth at EXCITE the next morning. The Patch had long since changed from her gay garb into one of her man-shirts (I never thought I'd say this but, *thank God!*). The Hinderance meandered to and fro fastidiously adjusting her fanny pack. *Who still wears fanny packs?* I wondered. Milton had managed to find the bar and seemed to be sipping on something quite un-manly, like a daiquiri via a straw—an egregious violation of Man Law #618. Harper was the last one to arrive. As she walked toward us, she looked as pale as a ghost or, at least, looked like she had seen one.

"What's wrong?" I mouthed.

"I'll send you a text in the cab," she whispered.

No sooner than settling on the back seat of the van which served as our communal cab, I got the following text from Harper:

[5:30] **Harper:** When I arrived to my room, there were 3 dozen red roses, strawberries dipped in chocolate and champagne waiting for me.
[5:30] **Nia:** Awwwww…Kent is so sweet. He misses his wife.
[5:30] **Harper:** Kent didn't send them.
[5:30] **Nia:** Well, who did?!
[5:30] **Harper:** Ummmm…Milton. :-\

My jaw dropped to the floor of the cab. That nasty bastard!

CHAPTER

—*——*—

7

There's no way to approach the complex and ogre-ish behavior that was our boss, Milton, except to dive directly into it. Milton gave 'Horrible' a bad name.

First of all, this middle-aged, dumpy Jewish dad thought he was a sexy womanizer. And that might be true, if he spent his days at an old folks' home. Surely fresh off being fired from his last job (we can't prove it, but are convinced that it was the case), Milton filled his days with shifting his responsibilities off to his staff and teetering the fine line of sexual harassment toward his mostly young female subordinates.

We invested an exorbitant amount of time trying to figure exactly what made him Vice-President material. He was not smart AND he embodied all of the qualities of the average child molester: sneaky, calculating and grimy-looking. The only accoutrement missing was the nondescript white van. Milton was superficial and seemed like the type of scheister who had enough patch-worked expertise from a variety of jobs well enough to look good on paper. Oh, Milton knew the game, and on this point, I must give him credit. Armed confidently with his version of professional decorum, Milton knew just where to interject the industry jargon so that he would not seem like an imbecile, how to riddle his subordinates with ridiculous and circuitous questions to deflect attention from his ineptitude, and was always, always, always sporting a used car salesman's grin. At Taking Chances! this made him golden. Insert picture of a creepy, older guy here.

[14:37] **Harper:** If Milton emails me in a demanding tone asking for one more thing I am going to lose it!

[14:37] **Harper:** Ugh!

[14:37] **Nia:** you have my permission to virtually shank Melvin.

[14:37] **Harper:** thank you!

[14:37] **Harper:** haha

[14:37] **Nia:** He is in rare form today. I'm still running his "stats". Why doesn't he leave me alone?!

[14:37] **Nia:** LOSER!

[14:37] **Nia:** I hate Milton Fonzarelli. If he knew what was best, he'd rid himself of that old school/Happy Days leather jacket. That's something he can focus on versus making us more miserable.

[14:38] **Harper:** He is a loser of epic proportions. He just sent me an email with the subject like "please send me…" and the body of the email contained a list of tasks he needed. No greeting, no closing just blah, blah, blah.

[14:38] **Harper:** Milton, do your own work

[14:38] **Nia:** Right, Milton. Beat it!*

*Note: *Beat it!* had become mine and Harper's dismissal du jour. It had a certain je na sais quoi: dainty, but forceful. Most of the losers at Taking Chances! had been recipients of the command and rightfully so because they deserved it. Ha!

Since Milton was such the skirt chaser and Taking Chances! had no HR manager, he was in Hog's Heaven. On several occasions, we observed him ogling the derrieres of shapely colleagues. Bold and inappropriate, he even had the nerve to stop in his tracks, make a 180 degree pivot and watch a woman walk away. Nasty. Bastard. There are no other words.

Strangely (tongue definitely in cheek), Milton took an acute interest in Harper and her "career," summoning her to his office repeatedly to assure her that her professional development was of the utmost importance to him. Yeah, effing, right. Let's be clear about something, Harper had no intention of making a career at Taking Chances! The cesspool was a bridge to something better... ummm...like being a lady who lunched. What else? We all knew this about her. Milton knew it, too, but was more interested in spending time taking in the eye-candy that was Harper.

Not very different from a chorus of 5th grade girls, a few of us office cool kids teased Harper that Milton was her work husband. I'm cracking up right now even thinking about it. She nearly vomited in her mouth at the thought, but took our joshing in great stride. There was no question about it; Harper was definitely Milton's favorite staff member, but for absolutely, positively all the wrong reasons. None of his interest in her had anything to do with her job performance or work ethic. Even though she wore a brave face, poor Harper was so uneasy and sometimes nervous that she'd be caught alone with him and he'd make his move.

[13:16] **Harper:** Eileen (Milton's assistant) had to go to lunch with Milton! Haaaa!
[13:18] **Nia:** Poor Eileen!!!
[13:18] **Harper:** I know! Better her than me.

[13:18] **Nia:** Sidebar: Milton was ogling you lovingly whilst we were chatting him up this morning. Yuck!
[13:18] **Harper:** Sick!
[13:19] **Harper:** Yeah, Milton..stop gazing at me and get our dysfunctional team in shape! You have bigger fish to fry!

Now you understand why Milton's basket of love sent to Harper's San Francisco hotel was not a surprise to me. My infinite wisdom—a.k.a loser radar—foreshadowed a gesture of this sort when I saw how smitten Milton seemed to be with Harper.

We had to devise a quick scheme.

As we were exiting the cab and entering the Stinking Rose, an Italian restaurant in the Bay Area, Harper and I managed to squeeze in a quick convo.

"Ha! I just saw your Facebook status from my phone. 'Dying inside?' That's clever," I teased.

"Well, that's how I feel. This is horrible!" said Harper. "What do I do? What do I say?"

"Right now…nothing," I advised. If we could get through dinner and back to the hotel, Harper and I could meet in one of our suites to figure out how to handle this all.

Thank God there was one thing that we could count on: Milton publicly putting on his dunce's cap.

In the middle of dinner, Milton blurted, "Harper, did you like the basket I sent to your room?"

The Patch and The Hinderance looked stunned. I, too, feigned surprise.

Milton continued, "I just wanted to send you a token of my appreciation and let you know that you're doing a good job. I hope you know that I want to do everything I can to ensure success in your career path."

Harper was able to muster a shaky 'Thanks' and the dinner went on like everything was normal. That couldn't have been further from being the case. Just when we thought Milton had reached an all-time low, he managed to trump himself. Repeatedly. Like an oblivious idiot.

As we were exiting the restaurant, Milton asked Harper if she'd like to walk back to the hotel with him instead of taking a cab. He really wanted to talk to her more about, guess what, her career path. He insisted that the 14 blocks wouldn't be *that* bad. Before Harper could protest, The Patch and The Hinderance said they'd LOVE to take the stroll with Milton.

Milton looked crestfallen and for a nanosecond, I actually felt sorry for him. Call me crazy, but I could have sworn that he and I connected telepathically at that moment and he said, "*Please don't stick me with these damn losers! Let me ride back with you and Harper.*" Quick on the draw, I shot back a mental, "*Ummm. Yeah. No.*", and proceeded to hail the next cab. "I think I'll share a cab with Nia. After all, Milton, 4 inch heels aren't exactly walking shoes! Next time, I'll wear my Rockports and we'll take that stroll," Harper teased.

The losers easily hoofed it down the hill back toward the hotel. After all (and to Harper's brilliant point), the walk would not be a problem for any of them since they were all sporting dreadful yet comfortable loafers. Desperate to rid ourselves of Milton and his brown-nosers, we hopped in our Ford AstroVan of a cab back to The Clift and rode back in silence for a change.

Yet another crisis averted. Double *phew*! It had been such the long night, but tomorrow would be a more eternal day.

Have you ever heard of Moscone West?

CHAPTER

8

The Moscone Center was the heartbeat of all large conventions which blew threw San Francisco. The luxurious facility boasted four separate buildings and its campus spanned approximately 50 city blocks. EXCITE drew attendees from around the globe who were seeking the latest education, vendors, and networking in the philanthropic and fundraising management. It afforded our team to liaise with several of our clients and peers in the industry.

Because Harper and I were responsible for our booth on the exhibit show floor, we spent most of our time in the Moscone West section of the convention center. Each morning, we walked two miles from our hotel to Moscone West because we had been forbidden by Taking Chances'!

Finance Manager so that we might save the company money. How cheap! With pedometers clipped to our uniform of black pants and itchy, Taking Chances! oxford shirts, we bitched and moaned each of the ten thousand steps.

By the time we arrived at Moscone West each day, we were angrier than a woman scorned. Our husbands weren't exactly thrilled about their wives walking the streets of San Francisco at dawn fending off beggars either.

Meeting us at EXCITE was our colleague, Jack Norb, who maintained the West Coast installation of Taking Chances! (read: his home office in Oakland). A passive-aggressive Queen, he tortured us from across the country with his barrage of useless ideas and threw temper tantrums when he couldn't have his way. Jack was designer-svelte (like almost all of the gay boys) and very rarely seen without a tailored shirt of Egyptian cotton, brushed nickel cuff links and a pair of Ferragamo loafers. What tickled Harper and me most was his affinity for tight-ass, flat-front pants which accentuated his…erra…package.

I saw "it" from clear across the exhibit hall.

Since I was muted from the sheer sight of "it," I had to send Harper a quick text. You see, even though we live in the 21st century, Taking Chances! had a strict policy against too much talking to fellow colleagues when working at trade shows…ummmmm, OK. No Human Resources department, but this is what they chose to focus on, this policy crafted by the oh-so-useless Sara, the VP of Nothing. *le sigh* But I digress…

[10:35] **Nia:** Ummm…does Jack have a sock in his pants?
[10:35]**Harper:** OMG…is that loser here already?
[10:35] **Nia:** Yep. Does he know how tight his pants are?
[10:35] **Harper:** Ewwwwww…I see them. How can those be comfortable?
[10:36] **Nia:** I am so embarrassed for him.
[10:36] **Nia:** He doesn't have enough pride to be ashamed for himself.

[10:36] **Harper:** Maybe if he knew that he looks like he's wearing leggings he might.
[10:37] **Nia:** I dare you to tell him!
[10:37] **Harper:** Hell will certainly freeze over first.

Just as we wrapped up our virtual conversation, Jack was upon us; fake euro-kisses and all. A minor celebrity at EXCITE, Jack used to actually work for the organization before he was lured away by Taking Chances!. I'm sure he rues the day that happened.

Barely done saying hello to us, he immediately began issuing orders. "What you all *NEED* to do is 'this'..." and "What the two of you *SHOULD* do is 'that'..." Harper and I were so over him within about 15 minutes.

Harper absolutely lost it when he "told" (not to be confused with "asked") her to move some boxes from the storage area of the convention hall to our exhibit booth; Jack's antics made Simon Cowell look like a choir boy. Having learned to read Harper like a book, I could see the fire brimming in her eyes. Within a split second, she asked Jack if they could step to the site and "chat" (this was Harper-ese for a good, old-fashioned cursing out). All I heard her say was this: "I am annoyed at the way you have glided in here on your parade float after Nia and I have spent the day doing back-breaking, manual labor. If you want the boxes moved, you will move them yourself! Am I clear?"

Jack was as red as a beet, and it was now clear to him that he didn't have the market cornered on theatrics. Harper had set him straight. I looked at him from the corner of my eye as he removed his cufflinks and schlepped a tower of boxes whilst pouting.

You could have heard a pin drop. He did an about-face and sashayed to the other side of the convention center at the speed of light.

As soon as he was out of sight, I shot a message to Harper.

[11:15] **Nia:** *high five*
[11:15] **Nia:** Am dying.
[11:15] **Harper:** Eat my dust, Tight Pants!

And with that, the balance of EXCITE was a breeze.

CHAPTER

When we returned to the office after enjoying two compensatory days following the San Francisco debacle (that was the least we were owed), gossip permeated the Taking Chances! suite. This was not a novel notion; there was always something afoot. An intra-office affair. A random layoff; Taking Chances'! passive-aggressive approach to firing those who the Senior Management Team did not have the cajones to rid themselves of outrightly. Another lost client. I must be honest: the gossip was usually worth the price of actually dragging ourselves into TC!

Ever the eager beaver (read: Facebook/Pinterest/Twitter addict), Harper most always arrived at work about thirty minutes earlier than official business hours. A creature of habit, she picked up our lattes, checked Gmail™, her mental blog roll, and Facebook before she entertained a stitch of work.

She pounced me like a youthful jackal as soon as I logged on to Gmail™ to report on the chatter she'd heard around the water cooler earlier that morning. Today's wagging tongues were courtesy of one of our slug of an IT guys, Ned. Ned was as lazy as the day was long. He spent the majority of his time eating fries, dodging his responsibilities and effing up the company's IT infrastructure. Taking Chances! must have found this guy dwelling in the recesses of the Earth. At the very least, he was kidnapped while roaming the campus of Universal Studios; for he was a dead-ass ringer for Shrek. The only difference was that the fairytale ogre was much more handsome, a tad shorter, and wore a belt. If I had a dollar for every time that I'd seen the crack of Ned's butt, I could retire from Taking Chances! and never be forced to seek employment again; that's a pretty nice nest egg, huh?

[9:20] **Harper:** Are you sad Ned is leaving ;)

[9:20] **Nia:** Ned is leaving?

[9:20] **Nia:** How do you know?!

[9:20] **Harper:** Check your email…STAT!

[9:21] **Nia:** Well….seeing as I've not gotten the email and based on all of the email-related problems that I HAVE had, good riddance, Ned.

[9:21] **Nia:** When was it sent?

[9:21] **Nia:** Troubleshooting on my own…

[9:21]**Harper:** Maybe we will get someone who does more than chat with his friends.

[9:21] **Nia:** Right.

[9:21] **Harper:** His last day is next Friday. As it turns out, his wife accepted a professorial position at a university and her acceptance of the position was contingent upon Ned being placed on the university's IT staff. Do they know he's clueless? They couldn't.

[9:22] **Nia:** Our loss is their gain…who cares? I do have one piece of advice for Ned: before he shows up for the first day at his new J-O-B: get thee to the Big & Tall Men's section.

[9:22] **Harper:** And make sure to purchase some BELTS

[9:22] **Nia:** 'Cause surely the folks at his new gig should not be subjected to the crack attacks and cascading gut as have we

[9:22] **Nia:** Do better, Ned. Do better.

[9:23] **Nia:** P.S. Still no email; begs me to wonder what else I'm missing. Let me log into Webmail. Drats!

[9:23] **Harper:** ugh, I don't understand why this is an issue EVERY DAY

[9:23] **Nia:** Ummmm…'cause Ned is too busy doing nothing. I want to be in on interviewing his replacement; I mean…can we get someone that knows what he's doing?

[9:23] **Harper:** seriously!

Before long, other sycophants drew our ire. It never took very long. Anyone who came to our side of the suite, was forced to pass mine and Harper's cubes. Folks usually tried to dart past without drawing our attention. Little did they know, we had eyes in the back of our heads and canine-like hearing abilities; we saw and heard EVERYTHING.

[10:13] **Harper:** Oh dear, Wilhelmina is getting MORE fashion advice from Mona.

[10:15] **Nia:** OMG!

[10:16] **Harper:** And, get this, there was mention made of leather pants.

[10:16] **Nia:** Hush your mouth! Well, Mona is the leather oracle in the office. Her biker-ish leather vest and pants that she dons on casual Fridays make her a subject matter expert.

[10:16] **Harper:** Some, I've decided, are hopeless.

[10:17] **Harper:** I predict that Willie and Mona will spontaneously combust in their leather/pleather.

[10:17] **Nia:** Please let me make sure I'm not close by; I can't afford to have my perfectly coiffed brows singed from my forehead.

Breathing the same air as the Willies, Monas, and Neds was more asphyxiating than a barbed-wire noose. I needed relief, and fast. I decided to call on the only person who could deliver me from this occupational hell. The only thing that could save me from hanging myself from my cubicle was the good Lord.

Are you there God, it's me, Nia? What have I done so absolutely dread-ful that I am STILL damned to Taking Chances!? What lesson are you trying to teach me? And why is it taking so long? You know that I've not the patience of Job. Please get me outta here before I lose it.

I promise I'll go to church on Sunday.

Not this Sunday, though. I have brunch with the girls.

You understand.

CHAPTER

✳ ———————— ✳

10

Thank God that He was still in the blessing business. As not to become a self-eating toxin, I knew I'd need to pursue other opportunities. Taking Chances! was forcing me to die a very slow death.

About the time when I thought I could take no more, I received a call from a former colleague who wondered if I would be interested in a director-level role within his communications agency. After exchanging a few e-mail messages, we scheduled an interview and Harper was among the first who I told (after Evan, of course). I managed to situate the interview that same week. I thought it went very well and couldn't wait to share. I think the chance of one of us escaping gave us both a glimmer of hope. But first things first, when I returned to the Taking Chances! Office, I passed a pitiful waif of a colleague in the hallway. Because she was virtually a Lilliputian, wore a layer-less bob, and dressed much like a fairytale character; Harper and I dubbed her "Little Lord Fauntleroy" or LLF (and pronounced *elf…*yes…elf).

[14:12] **Nia:** Ummm...
[14:12] **Nia:** Do you and the Elf have on the same dress?
[14:12] **Harper:** I think it's very similar (barf)
[14:12] **Nia:** The Elf looks like she's 55 years old but she's only 30, I think.
[14:13] **Harper:** Mine is Diane von Furstenberg and I don't even think the Elf knows who that is. Unfortunately, I thought I looked cute before I saw her.
[14:13] **Nia:** Bwahahahahah
[14:13] **Nia:** She definitely has no idea who DVF is
[14:13] **Nia:** I'm sure of it
[14:13] **Nia:** so...the job interview went well
[14:13] **Nia:** I'm just afraid that they might not be able to afford me
[14:13] **Harper:** oh really???
[14:13] **Nia:** Yeah:-(
[14:14] **Harper:** Oh no. That is a major bummer
[14:14] **Nia:** Yeah...it's disappointing
[14:14] **Nia:** Though it's miserable here, i have my habits
[14:14] **Nia:** and I can't make less money…my luxe shopping habits dictate the same.
[14:14] **Nia:** And to have to go some place and actually do real work
[14:14] **Nia:** But we'll see...
[14:14] **Nia:** They didn't say 'no'.
[14:15] **Harper:** so its still up for negotiation?
[14:15] **Nia:** i think so
[14:15] **Nia:** they're going to let me know by the end of this week

[14:15] **Nia:** I know one thing: they think I'm AWESOME...lol
[14:16] **Harper:** Isn't that a statement of the obvious?

Touché.

CHAPTER

✳ ———————— ✳

11

Each day, without fail, I tried to forcefully will myself to dig deeply within the abyss of my soul and make the best of being at Taking Chances!. Each day, without fail, I was forced to analyze my reality and my habits.

There was my financial contribution to my family's household. Evan thought I actually liked my J-O-B; I didn't have the heart to tell him otherwise. I drew a decent salary which allowed us to send our son to one of the toniest prep schools in the Southeast. Without it, The Boy would be damned to the public school system. Yeah. No. Not an option.

Evan had old-school sensibilities and the thought of me rocking the stability of our smoothly-sailing ship would send him into anaphylactic shock. If he was so old school, why couldn't I be the chocolate Betty Draper? You know...the Stepford Wife.

Because I also worship at the thrones of style and fashion, my affinity for all things luxe: Gucci, Manolo Blahnik, Louis Vuitton, and Mercedes held me hostage to Taking Chances! I had been blessed with a discerning eye, but cursed without a silver spoon in my mouth, so I had tons of bills, bills, bills. It's downright pitiful, and I know it. Hey! Don't judge me. I know, you don't EVEN have to say it; there's a seat in a 12-Step program some place waiting just for me.

It had all become crystal clear; my misery boiled down to a paper chase. How antithetical to my sheer being. In a million years, I would have never thought that I would buckle to the all-mighty dollar. I was accustomed to a certain lifestyle, and I wasn't willing to give it up just yet. It's sad, but it's so. "To thine own self be true," right?

Do you want to hear what's worse? Well...there was this tiny matter called a global recession. Though I hated work, it was a steady check. Due to the economic climate, every other person I knew had either been affected directly or knew someone who had been downsized and/or couldn't find a job. As bold and brazen of an individual as I am, I liked security and tried to avoid the pitfall of becoming a statistic. A student of life, I understand the law of economics; what goes up must eventually come down. Seriously...I get it. I, however, wasn't prepared (mentally or financially) to draw up the nerve to take a calculated risk.

I always thought I was too smart to be caught up in this matrix. What was I going to do to get out of it?

Maybe Milton *was* right when I, in a fleeting moment of weakness, expressed my challenges with Taking Chances'! corporate culture. "Hang in there," he encouraged, "We're all experiencing a bit of ennui here and there. After all," he chuckled, "no one else is hiring right now anyway."

Unfortunately, I knew he was telling the truth.
Jackass.

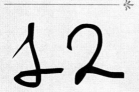

"Maybe it's me," I began to think.

Seriously.

Maybe *I'm* the problem.

Though I'd been downsized in my two previous positions (that was the nature of the beast), there was a Barry, a Sarah, a Milton, a Patch in every office that I'd worked in. It didn't take me long to identify the lemmings. Before long, said lemmings were grating my last nerve.

[14:23] **Nia:** Is it me?
[14:23] **Harper:** What?
[14:23] **Nia:** You know…am I abnormal? Why can't I get

into this place? Some people come here, bop around and make it seem like we work at Disney…the place where magic happens.

[14:23] **Harper:** Nia, we've been through this a million times.

[14:23] **Nia:** This I know but I'm feeling helpless. Like I want to slit my wrists. I can't believe that I've gotten trapped in another dead-end job.

[14:23] **Harper:** Is your Last Will and Testament up to date?

[14:23] **Nia:** Ummm, yeah. How morbid! Why do you ask?

[14:23] **Harper:** Before you slit your wrists, did you bequeath those David Yurman bangles to me? I need to figure how hard I need to push you over the cliff.

[14:23] **Nia:** *speechless*

[14:24] **Harper:** I don't know why you're allowing these TC! losers to mess with your head.

[14:24] **Nia:** I know, I know.

[14:24] **Harper:** Before long, you will have moved on to your new job. By the way, have you heard anything from them recently? Based on how well you said the interview went, hopefully they'll be ringing you up soon.

[14:30] **Harper:** And when they do, you'd better look out for me! I can't imagine being here without you for long.

[14:30] **Nia:** How sweet of you to say! And to think that six minutes ago you wanted me dead. You know…for the bangles.

[14:30] **Harper:** I confess: I am a materialistic bee-yotch. You know that's why you love me.

[14:31] **Nia:** True dat.

CHAPTER

※————————————————————————————※

13

Harper was apparently clairvoyant.

The company that I interviewed with a couple of weeks earlier did call. When I got home that evening, there was a message on my voicemail from their recruiter. The recruiter must have a Ph.D. in Opacity. Like a maniac, I played the message over and over again hoping that I'd glean something that I didn't hear in the twenty-nine previous times that I'd hit #3 for "hear this message again."

> "Hi, Nia. This is Rosemary from XYZ Media. I'm so sorry that it took me a while to get back to you. I was on holiday, had an Inbox of nearly 300 messages when I returned and my daughter has had swine flu all this

week (thinking to myself: Is she serious? TMI!). *Anyway, I wanted to talk to you a little more about the position; everyone loved you and thinks that you'd be a great fit for the team. Please give me a call tomorrow because my son is in a play at his school on Friday, and I've volunteered as an usher for the encore presentation of the play* (again…thinking to myself: TMI); *so, I won't return to the office until Monday. OK? I can't wait to talk to you. Bye.*"

I began to do what I sometimes do best; obsess. What'd she mean by, "…you'd be a great fit for the team?" Was an offer pending? Did they think I'd be a great fit for the team, BUT something is holding them back from making a decision right now? Aaarrrrgggggghhh!

Before long, I settled down. OK, OK…a couple of martinis… extra dirty…were involved. It's amazing how Bombay Sapphire can be such a calming agent. I relaxed my mind and prepared for whatever the next day had in store for me.

There's one problem: the road to hell is paved with good intentions.

I didn't sleep a wink that night.

CHAPTER

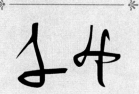

14

[8:55] **Nia:** They called.

[8:55] **Harper:** They did?! Why didn't you call me last night?

[8:55] **Nia:** Their recruiter left a message. I returned her call on my way in this morning; so the ball is in her court.

[8:56] **Harper:** Well, keep me posted. I'm thinking good thoughts.

[8:56] **Nia:** Thanks, Doll.

[9:34] **Harper:** Anywho...have you seen Carla's slut outfit?

[9:34] **Nia:** Yeah. I saw her slinking by.

[9:35] **Harper:** She is just the perfect stereotype of TRASHY

[9:35] **Harper:** I mean, why is she wearing that summer-thin skirt and skimpy sweater?

[9:35] **Nia:** Last time I checked, it was twenty degrees outside.

[9:35] **Harper:** It's one of the cheapest outfits that I've ever seen in my life.

[9:37] **Nia:** *saying a prayer that Carla does not catch walking pneumonia* 'Cause I do like her even though she dresses like the Mom on Harper Valley PTA.

Rosemary the Recruiter and I finally caught up with each other. After exchanging pleasantries and a preview of her pre-school son's play, we got down to business. XYZ Media had made an offer. No somersaults yet, please. They could only afford to pay me $20,000 less than I was making at Taking Chances! and that was on the high end of their scale, but there was a mix of benefits (not actual bonuses) that could contribute toward making a difference.

The Devil That I Knew, Taking Chances!, was looking pretty good all of a sudden.

[10:45] **Nia:** They can't afford me and I can't afford to take what they're offering.

[10:46] **Harper:** I'm so sorry.

[10:46] **Nia:** Can we grab a 'rita at lunch? I'm depressed. Boo hoo hoo.

[10:46] **Harper:** I'll give you the balance of the day to be depressed but after that, pick yourself up and start over again. *passing my virtual (and monogrammed, of course) handkerchief*

[10:46] **Nia:** *pouting*

[10:46] **Harper:** Seriously. Repeat after me: "We're better than this place."

[10:46] **Nia:** grumblegrumblegrumble

[10:46] **Harper:** Grumble all you want but say it!

[10:46] **Nia:** *teeth clenched*

[10:47] **Harper:** As much as your parents paid for orthodontia, you'd better stop grinding those molars.

[10:47] **Nia:** *through my teeth* We're better than this place.
[10:48] **Nia:** grumblegrumblegrumble
[10:48] **Harper:** Let's sneak out at 1130; this calls for a two-hour lunch.
[10:48] **Nia:** Word.

CHAPTER

✳————————✳

15

Before long, the anniversary of my hire rolled around. No performance review. No mention of a review. Par for the course.

Only because I began to harass him, Milton didn't get around to actually scheduling it until just before the December holidays. Six weeks after it was due. I wasn't exactly looking forward to it. In a staff meeting a month earlier, Barry announced that a freeze had been placed on all possible merit increases.

My review was glowing; I considered it an adult report card. Under normal circumstances, positive feedback was my coup de grat. My goal was to do well enough to be promoted to a director-level position. This, at least, gave me something to strive toward.

Oh what a difference a performance review makes....

Despite busting my butt without reward, I was not advanced to the next level on the organizational chart. Something about my leaving at 5:30 every day (the official and published end of the business day at Taking Chances! Go figure.) and the *perception* that I was not a team player...huh??!

As you can likely imagine, this maligned accusation got under my skin a bit, but at least I had gainful employment. So long as no one asked me to do much more than was required and my payroll check posted on the 1st and 15th each each month, I was OK. I decided that I couldn't do any better. Milton had spoken it into existence.

Jackass.

Fucking jackass.

CHAPTER

✳ ———————————— ✳

16

When I emerged from shock a couple of days later, I actually got mad. So mad, in fact, that I implemented my own "Do Nothing" campaign. Was it the most mature approach? Surely not. Did it make me feel better about my lot in life? Bet your bottom dollar, it did.

My "Do Nothing" campaign consisted of doing just that: a whole lot of nothing. Don't get me wrong. I'm not stupid, so to be more precise, I must admit I did *mostly* nothing. Colossal difference. Since Milton had become paranoid about the security of his *own* job lately (it was obvious that he wasn't making his departmental numbers and his staff hated him so much that we were on the verge of staging a mutiny), he didn't quite have time to focus on what I was doing…the bare minimum. My days began to consist of sending requisite e-mail, reading various and sundry blogs, shopping on-line and watching the clock.

This behavior went on for some time before I became disgusted with myself. Here I was, in the prime of my professional life committing career suicide. It wasn't fair to Taking Chances! and it certainly wasn't fair to me. Not so long ago, I considered myself brilliant, dynamic and the prototype of a team player. Choosing to become a victim of my circumstances had made me bitter, unfocused and a curmudgeon. I sported a permanent scowl, kept mostly to myself and only engaged with colleagues (loser-ish or not) when spoken to and would venture to say that I was depressed.

"How could I allow myself to sink into this black hole?" I asked myself.

I had no where to turn…or so I thought.

CHAPTER

※ ——————— ※

17

At my wit's end one day, I stumbled upon an article on Monster.com, a job-search portal. The headline spoke directly to me: *How To Tell If You're In The Wrong Job.* The article began with a quiz. "Do you daydream about your ideal job?" *Yes.* "Are you generally unfocused in your job?" *Hell, yes!* "Do you feel that you are using the strengths that won over the hiring manager for your job?" *Hell, no!* The quiz confirmed what I already knew; I was in the wrong job. What's new? As I read deeper into the article, though, it challenged the reader to perform an assessment of their strengths and weaknesses and gave tips about how to either cope or move on. I was interested in the latter. I thought I'd given it the old-college try with the coping mechanisms: deep breaths, conversations with my manager, yada, yada, yada. Skipping over *that* part of the article was so typically Nia. I needed a revelation, and I needed one quickly.

Since I wasn't doing anything else, I went old-school: I whipped out a legal pad and drew a line down the middle of one of the pages. On the left of the line I wrote "Strengths" and to the right of the line, I wrote "Weaknesses."

Strengths	Weaknesses
* Smart	* Moody
* Funny	* Emotional
* Leader	* Hate Losers
* Compassionate	* Detests Disorganization
* Resourceful	* Prefers to work in
* Team-Player	independently/in a silo
* Hard-Worker (just not	(read: HATES losers)
today)	
* Great Writer	
* Excellent Communicator	
(unless you are a getting	
on my nerves; read:	
HATES Losers)	

The handwriting was on the wall. I'd never seen it so powerfully displayed. Who knew that a couple of lists would be my road map? Can't you see it? Sure you do. I promise you, it's not written in invisible ink. I'd suppressed it so much that I had squeezed the life out of it. I almost didn't see it either.

Was God playing some sort of trick on me? I *know* I promised that I'd go to church, but I just hadn't *quiiiittteee* gotten around to doing so yet. Great. That's all I needed: The Big Guy's wrath. In the midst of my convoluted life, there was clarity. Though a holy roller I am not, I instantly remembered a Bible verse that I'd always loved, "Write a vision and make it plain.... It will come to pass at the appointed time…" Paying attention in Sunday School was actually paying off.

Instantly, my life was about to turn upside down.

Evan would be worried sick. My parents would think I, a normally logically thinking adult, had reverted back to my fly-by-the-seat-of-my-pants-ish teenaged ways. A "talking to" was in my immediate future from all three of them. But hadn't they taught me to follow my dreams? Wasn't it they who instilled faith within me? Maybe the joke was on them.

I could hardly wait to tell someone.

[15:25] **Nia:** I've figured out what I want to be when I grow up. Just right now. At 35 years old.
[15:26] **Harper:** Do tell!
[15:26] **Nia:** Are you ready?
[15:26] **Harper:** If you don't spit it out, I'm going to scale the walls of this horrid cube farm and choke you.
[15:26] **Nia:** A writer. There. I said it.
[15:26] **Harper:** It took you this long to figure that out? Stevie Wonder can see that you're a great writer.
[15:26] **Nia:** Awwww. Thank you, Grasshopper.
[15:27] **Harper:** Have you mentioned anything about this to Evan?
[15:27] **Nia:** Not yet. I'm not sure how he's going to respond. *wincing* 'Cause I think I want to do it full time.
[15:27] **Harper:** Sorry, girl, but Evan is going to shit a brick. Get your pooper scooper ready.
[15:27] **Nia:** I know but I'm going to be terribly unhappy unless I get this out of my system. I'm either going to do really, really well at writing or kick rocks (highly unlikely but possible).
[15:27] **Harper:** I wish I could persuade you otherwise but you're absolutely right.
[15:28] **Nia:** Will you be my number one fan? Read all of my books? Suggest them to your fancy schmancy book club?
[15:28] **Harper:** I believe in you, Doll. You've said it best and I agree:

you're clearly too brilliant for this place. After all, I've already figured what I'll wear on your media tour.

From this day forward, with a nudge from my dear Harper, I was a different Nia.

Nia, the Writer.

Nia, the Writer, with clarity.

Nia, the Writer, with clarity, a stack of loans AND a weakness for Louboutins.

Damn.

Riddle me this: does clarity pay bills? OK...don't answer that.

Crossroads suck.

CHAPTER

18

I knew I had some things to think about on my ride home. I plugged in my iPod and allowed my thoughts to stream alongside the melodies of The Black Eyed Peas. *"I've got feeling...that tonight's gonna be a good night"*, crooned frontman Will.I.Am.

Yeah, right. Not in the mood. Power off.

I was five miles away from my moment of reckoning. Evan had sent a text message that he was headed home from the office early and would begin dinner. I had five miles to figure this out; seven if I went the long way. The long way it is!

There I was: alone with my thoughts. Great.

I wasn't quite sure how Evan would react. Since he was

the poster child for cool, calm and collected, his poker face had always thrown me for a loop. We'd had a wonderful ten-year marriage; as solid as a rock but it hadn't always been blissful in the areas of our finances. We'd gone through a couple of layoffs in the last five years but always managed to keep our heads above water. Our motto was: "We can get through anything. Together." Revealing to Evan that I wanted to quit my job and become a writer just might test the strength of our vows. I'd be giving up a six-figure salary without the guarantee that I'd ever draw another red-cent for payroll.

I rehearsed my schpiel nearly a thousand times and mentally staged every scenario possible but finally decided that I'd go with the 'straight-no chaser' approach. I'd tell Evan that I wanted to take a year off to organize myself and pursue this writing thing. I would utilize my savings (the little that I had set back when I wasn't purchasing $800 stilettos) to pay my personal bills. If he could swing the household bills with his salary, I would have no expenses and would agree to a shopping moratorium during this time. I'd *cringing* do my own hair, manicures and pedicures. Since the lease was nearly up on my BMW, I'd opt for a smaller car without a loan. All of this seemed fair.

As I turned into our subdivision, I felt great about my plan. If Evan was on board, I'd draft my letter of resignation tonight. Oh, it'd be such a burden lifted. I could finally see beyond Taking Chances! I was breathing a bit easier already. Things were looking up professionally and I stuck out my chest a little. Did I want to write a novel?, I self-queried. Freelance for magazines? Both? Yes! My creative juices were a-flowin'.

When I turned into our garage, I felt like a million bucks. After parking, I turned the iPod to one of my theme songs, Mary J Blige's "Just Fine" and danced to it in the seat of my car. When the song was done and after I'd waved my hands in the air; waved them like I just didn't care, I was so optimistic that I was almost inspired to execute a Charlie Chaplin-ish side kick. Almost.

After passing through the foyer, I found Evan waiting for me in the parlor. The knot in his tie was loosened and the top button of dress shirt was undone. His elbows rested on his knees and his hands were clasped. Much out of the ordinary, Evan's poker face looked…well…sad and somewhat distressed.

Before I could muster a "What's wrong, Honey?", I heard Evan say: "Nia, I was just laid off from my job."

Ever the dutiful wife, I reached to hug and comfort him but all I could think was I'd never escape Taking Chances! now. My newly-found dreams flew out of the window. I felt suffocated and could only manage the strength to sob and sob and sob. I could hardly catch my breath.

My professional crossroads had just become a troll bridge…riddled again with Taking Chances! losers.

Instantly. (Get it?)

Damn.

THE *Instantly!* JOB RESIGNATION TEST

Answer the questions below by selecting the response that BEST applies to you. Be honest! This is now a test. Be reflective! Think about the big picture rather than what happened yesterday or last week.

1-6 'Yes' responses — Do not make any hasty decisions. Give yourself at least 3 months to improve your attitude. Attempt to be the catalyst for change.

7-12 'Yes' responses — Haul ass. It's that simple.

#	*Statement*	*Response*	
1	Does your dissatisfaction with your current job make you moody and overly critical of others?	Yes No	O O
2	Are you uncomfortable talking with your Human Resources Partner about "touchy" issues, whether they involve you or not, for fear of retaliation?	Yes No	O O
3	Is your productivity on any given day negatively impacted by your overall workplace attitude?	Yes No	O O
4	Do you dread the thought of having to come to work on Tuesday before going to work on Monday?	Yes No	O O
5	Although you understand the value of teamwork, do you ever feel appreciated for your individual contributions?	Yes No	O O
6	Does your manager meet with you regularly to give you both productive and constructive feedback?	Yes No	O O

#	*Statement*	*Response*	
7	When feedback is given, is it timely, validated by specific examples?	Yes No	◯ ◯
8	Do you feel your salary is commensurate with your work performance?	Yes No	◯ ◯
9	Are "on-time" performance evaluations an expectation of your organization?	Yes No	◯ ◯
10	Are there those within your work group who tend to make you feel uncomfortable because of things they say or do?	Yes No	◯ ◯
11	Do you have any input in the day-to-day decisions involving you and your work team?	Yes No	◯ ◯
12	Are periodic meetings held with the work team to keep all team members abreast of what the other is doing?	Yes No	◯ ◯

About The Author,
Shameeka Ayers

A corporate girl for nearly fifteen years, Shameeka Ayers married her love of marketing and public relations with her obsession with new media to create her alter ego, blog and brand, The Broke Socialite™, in 2006. Through this newly-found voice, Shameeka has utilized social media to create a series of highly-lauded dessert festivals called Sugar Coma Events™. She also produces lavish!™, a lifestyle bloggers' conference for those who utilize social media to engage about interior design, style, travel, food & wine, entertaining and other general lifestyle considerations. Shameeka made her "Exit, Stage Left" from corporate America in 2010 and is a highly sought after motivational speaker about her transition from employee to unlikely entrepreneur.

CPSIA information can be obtained at www.ICGtesting.com
Printed in the USA
BVOW031622200612

293226BV00006B/22/P

9 780976 273899